Only a Woman Could, and She did

by Dean Hodel

Only a woman could, and she did

CHAPTER ONE

"A man's gift maketh room for him, and bringeth him before great men."
- Proverbs 18.16

In a time where there are so many changes and opportunities, I've seen women with great potential get overlooked or ignored. Even in today's time, women still face the uphill battle of equal pay for equal work and trying to dispel ingrained stereotypes that prohibit their growth in certain business sectors. Facing those daily challenges could wear a person down and make them give up hope before taking their first step. During my life, I've witnessed women stand against those odds. Their struggles didn't result in the tipping point changes that movies were made about like Erin Brockovich or the women of Hidden Figures but, those women laid a path for others to follow. That path is constantly being reinforced by so many that it would be impossible to mention them all but, I noticed they all shared the same qualities, that are embodied by all women. These virtues have been recorded in the Bible since the time of Christ.

I often notice when I hear quotes from the Bible about women, they highlight their purity, their silent strength or duty to family. I thought it was time to highlight some other qualities women in the Bible had. The qualities that I've seen. These other qualities don't conflict with the ones we're used to talking about but, I think they give a fuller picture of the characteristics that women possess. Those characteristics can be the modern-day LIFE-TOOLS that are gifts from the creator for women.

So let's dispel some myths and rediscover

the gifts.

CHAPTER TWO

Often we see women standing on the precipice of the decision should they " ask or not to ask in meetings." There was an understanding that after every meeting the women would have a second meeting. In the second meeting amongst peers they felt comfortable with, they would ask questions. Contrary to their thoughts, their questions weren't basic, nor were they common knowledge. After the questions had been vetted in their safe space, you'd often see emails go out with those questions. Those emails would stimulate conversation, to look at new options in some cases. Sometimes those questions motivated others to clarify what the goals and intentions of the meeting were.

If those questions had been asked during the meeting, the impact and benefit would have been immediate. Be bold, ask your questions in the meeting. Let everyone put a face to the question. Knowing how to ask questions isn't just limited to meetings. Women need to be able to ask questions about benefits and career paths. For those who would discourage these actions and say it flies in the face of silent strength and dignity women should embody, we need only look at Mathew 15:21-27. This scripture speaks of the faith of the Canaanite woman. This scripture is often seen as controversial due to the lines 25- 27, where Jesus seems to compare the woman to a dog. However, we need to really look at what Jesus is saying to the Canaanite woman and the audacity and strength the woman displayed.

The woman had a question. Could someone heal her child? She had no connections. She wasn't on the list. If the disciples were the only boys club, she wasn't a member. When she approached the disciples, they shunned her. They shunned her because she wasn't of their faith. For all intensive purposes, she had no recourse, and she should have left. In all things, there is a choice. Historically, women have left the room, not participated in the conversation. They were stonewalled into silence. They didn't all leave on their own accord. Many doors have been physically and metaphorically slammed in women's faces. The Canaanite woman shows perseverance in the face of the wall of disciples. She continues to try to get Jesus's attention. She has a question. She has a purpose, and she will not be denied.

Finally, she is able to get the attention of Jesus. The Canaanite woman walks into a situation where the disciples are already mocking her before she can even plead her case. She is being dismissed before she has said a word. Take note, asking a question may cause others to disparage your name before they even hear your words. You may be judged lacking, for even wanting to speak in certain arenas. Others may think your requests have no place in those meetings. There will even be those who think you should be happy to be at the meeting but, shouldn't speak.

The Canaanite woman is in Jesus's presence and trusting his disciple's judgment, Jesus seeks to nip this encounter in the bud before it even takes place. Jesus says " I was only sent to the lost sheep of Israel." Still, the Canaanite woman is not dissuaded. "Lord Help me!". In what some may perceive as the ultimate public rebuttal Jesus says "It is not right to take the children's bread and toss it to their dogs." Again, take note, in the face of opposition, and it may be very public opposition keep your focus. It seems to be the nature of woman to not cause a scene and to be the ones that comfort others. When women are met with public derision or aggression, it can cause many women to retreat to a place of safety and calm. The Canaanite woman doesn't retreat, but she doesn't lose her grace or dignity.

The Canaanite woman displays another ability that women cultivate. The power of the tongue. The Canaanite woman doesn't cry, she doesn't run away, and she doesn't throw anything instead she replies to Jesus in a curt, short and witty way. Her reply stops those around her with its boldness and exhibits her intellect and perseverance. She says " but even the dogs eat the crumbs that fall from the master's table." This statement is powerful and succinct. She asks the Lord for help Jesus says "it's not for you but for the lost children of Israel." She then points out that she doesn't even need a full portion of the children of Israel she understands that the power in a slice of bread is present in a crumb. The revelation impresses Jesus, and he tells the disciples to move so she can sit at the table.

The Canaanite woman had a question. She needed to be heard. She didn't have to yell to be heard, and she didn't have to show out in a way she would regret, or that was inappropriate or "unprofessional." The Canaanite woman used a weapon woman harness daily. Women traditionally verbally communicate more. When brute strength has failed them, the power of their words has slain men. Let's take a lesson from the Canaanite woman, dare to speak until you are heard.

CHAPTER THREE

Many things can be said about the woman at the well, but I think we would all agree she had no problem speaking up. It's one of the most meaningful and entertaining texts depicting Jesus interacting with a woman. Here we see that Jesus has gone out of his way to meet the woman at the well. This is no chance encounter. This is a message for women to women. The lack of public recognition doesn't mean you haven't been noticed. Change is slow but when the moment comes you need to be prepared.

The woman at the well is sure of herself and what she can do. Jesus says "Give me a drink."

She replies "How is it that You, being a Jew, ask a drink from me, a Samaritan woman?". Let's look at the lesson being taught in this line. The woman at the well knows who she is. She knows where she stands on the world stage and in her town. Be aware of who is around you and what their title is. Understanding the culture and the climate in your workplace is not a necessary skill you need to master.

Later in this text, Jesus says "Whoever drinks of this water will thirst again. (referring to the water in the well), but whoever drinks of the water that I shall give him will never thirst." She replies "Sir, give me this water, that I may not thirst, nor come here to draw." The lesson here is when opportunities come, do not be afraid to ask for them. The other lesson here knows what you are asking for. Jesus offered an opportunity. The woman at the well asked for the opportunity, articulated what she was going to get and evaluated how it would improve her situation. If someone comes and offers an "opportunity" make sure you know what you are getting and how it will help you. Too often the "opportunity" of more money is offered and what you wind up with is more work, less time for yourself and family and more responsibility all without title or recognition. I've seen the money used as a false lure. By understanding the pros and cons of a situation, you'll have the clarity of the woman at the well.

The next exchange between Jesus and the woman at the well is a place I've seen many women challenged. Jesus says "Go call your husband.". This question is aimed at her eventful past. One of the most prevalent differences I see between men and women are how they handle their past. A lot of men shrug off the past adventures of their youth as a rite of passage or just things happen. In the same vein, a lot of women carry their past like penance around their necks. Women wear it as if past performance is an indicator of future events. Instead, women should own it, grow from it and move the conversation along. If women don't manage the past, it will manage them and become the elephant in the room.

The woman at the well doesn't freeze up or shrink into herself when Jesus brings up the subject of a husband. Instead, she confirms it.

" I have no husband." Then Jesus replies to that with the following details saying " you have well said, ""I have no husband,"' for you have had five husbands, and the one you now have is not your husband, in that you spoke truly." From Jesus' response, we can see the woman at the well has had and is currently having a questionable relationship. Yet, she doesn't dwell on those things. In the next sentence, she doesn't even address her past or present situation with a man but, moves on to confirm Jesus is a prophet. She hasn't lost sight of the opportunity. When a woman's past is brought up too often, they hide in shame and guilt. The lesson the woman at the well teaches, accept the past but keep the focus on the opportunity in front.

The woman at the well is the second step. Own your past and embrace the opportunity in front of you. Don't let your past learning moments discourage you. Those lessons or growing moments should be put in your toolbox as a reference. When someone brings them up to don't shy away from the stories. Your past stories have brought you to where you are now. When the past is brought up don't run from it, own them and keep moving toward the goal.

CHAPTER FOUR

The story of the woman with the issue of blood is a common story to us all. We need to look at what lessons the woman with the issue of blood teaches. First, we have to look at the state the woman with the issue of blood is in. The scripture says that the woman had an issue for 12 years. She had gone to every physician to be healed. This line is important to understand that the woman identified her problem. Then, she sought help. Too often women have challenges, instead of finding solutions they tend to endure. While faith sometimes requires us to stand, we, men and women, all want to make sure we do all we can live in the natural world. When we've done that, God takes it and handles it in the supernatural. This woman had to speak up about her condition like the Canaanite. She had to ignore her past experiences and embrace new opportunities like the woman at the well. For twelve years she pushed on and looked for a cure. By seeking out other physicians, she was keeping her eyes on the opportunities in front of her.

What else is there to do? You've spoken up, and you've been noticed. You've accepted your past. You're also embracing new opportunities that come your way. However, unfair it is women have to be twice as good at what they do, and they must be brave. The woman with the issue of blood takes the next step. She doesn't just embrace opportunities as they appear she thinks outside of the box. She tries something different than the rest of the group. The scripture says she came from behind and touched the border of his garment. These actions speak of how she was in the crowd but wasn't of the crowd. While people who saw Jesus just wanted to be in his presence and to behold him, this woman had a different plan. She knew if she touched him her problems would be solved. Often women come up with new innovative ideas that manifest as a direct result of their life experiences. When a problem is brought to a meeting, fresh look is required. There is a saying, it says the mind that made a problem, can't fix the problem. Women bring new perspectives and views to the table. Make sure your views make it to the meeting in the boardroom and not the meeting at lunch.

The scripture says she did this, touched the hem of his garment, and immediately her blood stopped. Then Jesus said, "Who touched me?". When you have an idea that is out of the box or not proven, own it. There have been so many stories of women who have thought of alternative paths to accomplish a task and feared the backlash of suggesting a plan at all. Sometimes women have come up with plans that others have owned as their own. This part of the scripture gives women the leeway to own what they have done. When Jesus asks who touched me, it is not to rebuke or punish but to complement and marvel. In today's market, every idea you have may not be a winner but own them and be brave, so others will know you are an innovator.

In the final portion of the scripture, Jesus says "Daughter be of good cheer, your faith has made you well. Go in peace." Here we see Jesus congratulating the woman, more importantly, he makes an acknowledgment. Jesus acknowledges that the woman with the issue of blood had the ability within herself to heal herself. Too many women don't give themselves enough credit when it comes to solving issues. It is a good thing to be humble and to spread the credit around when it is due. However, I've seen more women abdicate from taking any credit and stand on the side as others bask in the glow of their accomplishments. Jesus's words should be taken to heart. Know the answer is already in you. It is your unique perspective or approach to an issue which holds the answer. When you solve it, make sure you're not afraid to claim it.

CHAPTER FIVE

The story of Lazarus is one that has been retold from different points of view. Traditionally, Lazarus will serve as the example that Jesus can raise the dead. We will look at this story to uncover what message it is sending to women. We want to start examining the situation from Mary and Martha's point of view. They knew there was a problem. They called for Jesus when things were looking grim. They went ahead and embraced opportunity when they called upon Jesus not as a savior but as a friend to their brother. We find that the women were proactive in keeping Jesus abreast of the situation even unto the day Lazarus died. Still, Jesus did not come until Lazarus had passed.

The text says that as soon as Martha heard Jesus was coming, she went to meet him. We can't know for sure what is going on in Martha's mind, but we can give her credit for thinking outside of the box. Martha might have been going to demand that Jesus do something which everyone thought was an impossibility. Lazarus had been laid to rest four days. The number of days is important as it is the Jewish thought that the spirit lingers around the body for three days after death. If Martha was going to ask Jesus to do something, we know that something would have to be the miracle of raising her brother. Also, take note, women have no problems requesting miracles from Jesus. Or Martha is going to unleash her grief against Jesus. We don't see a lot of people going to Jesus to tell him he has failed. We can't know which one she had in mind, but we do know, her going up to meet Jesus set her apart. Everyone else is waiting for Jesus to come, Martha breaks rank and goes to Jesus.

Martha goes to Jesus and says these famous words. "Lord, if you had been here my brother would not have died. But even now I know whatever you ask of God. God will give it." Here Martha says what Jesus can do and then says he could still fix this issue with her brother. This scripture is usually interpreted as how faithful Martha is. When she uses the words "even now," it shows that even in the face of death she believes Jesus can overcome it.

There is another way to look at this text that makes it more so applicable to women today. Martha is aware of the capabilities of Jesus, and she calls on him to fix it. When things go wrong women need to know who can really address the issue. Often the person who could fix a problem may be busy or not understand how vital they are to a situation. In crisis moments like these, the person who can address the issue needs to be identified and directed to the situation to address. What would have happened if Martha would have said? "Jesus, thanks for coming. Let me show you to a seat, and you can watch from there." With words like that Martha makes no demands on Jesus and she doesn't exercise her faith. When women don't hold people accountable to their word, simple projects can balloon into a chaotic mess. I know there is some hesitation to hold people accountable. When people are held accountable sometimes they push back. Those people go on the defensive, wanting to know who left you in charge. Accountability isn't about who is the boss, as it is about who should be responsible for their part.

When Martha says "even now" Jesus responds and says "your brother will rise again." Don't assume the response to holding people accountable, will be negative. We find in some cases that just being that reminder is enough, to get a person to fulfill their part of the project or bargain. There are so many ways accountability is tracked in our society from to do lists, to outlook reminders to meeting prompts on our phones. Making people accountable isn't a nuisance. Reminding people of their part of a project isn't bossy. Life is running faster than we are and sometimes we need to have a person who won't hesitate to remind us of the role we play and our responsibility. People's view will change towards you when you have the information of who is supposed to do what and when. It will also bring to the forefront in an indisputable way the added value you bring to a team.

CHAPTER SIX

"For I know the thoughts that I think toward you, saith the LORD, thoughts of peace, and not of evil, to give you an expected end."

- Jeremiah 29.11

We've looked at four popular stories in the Bible. I want to suggest to you that they are a guide from Jesus. They exemplify the strength, courage and innovative thinking women have had since time in memoriam. While women take a stand for their rights, it's also time for men to speak and bear witness to their struggle. There are social customs and business stereotypes that try to pigeon-hole women into roles that will use their gifts without giving them the credit for their work.

These four stories speak to four steps great women have taken in the Bible. These women have spoken up, embraced opportunities, owned their past without shame or explanation, thought outside the box, been proactive and held people accountable. Take some time and see how the creator has given these examples of the potential in all women. Most of all these stories tell of events that only a woman could have done, and in all of her glory, she did.

Embracing your potential passes your gifts on to the next generation.

CHAPTER SEVEN

Dare to Ask (Mathew 15:21-27)(NKJV)

21 Leaving that place, Jesus withdrew to the
region of Tyre and Sidon. 22 A Canaanite
woman from that vicinity came to Him, crying
out, "Lord, Son of David, have mercy on me!
My daughter is suffering terribly from demon-
possession."
23 Jesus did not answer a word. So his
disciples came to Him and urged Him, "Send
her away, for she keeps crying out after us." 24
He answered, "I was only sent to the lost sheep
of Israel."
25 The woman came and knelt before Him.

"Lord, help me!" she said. [26] He replied, "It is
not right to take the children's bread and toss it
to their dogs." [27] "Yes, Lord," she said, "but
even the dogs eat the crumbs that fall from
their master's table."
[27] Then Jesus answered, "Woman, you have
great faith! Your request is granted." And her
daughter was healed from that very hour.

File the past and embrace Opportunity (John 4:1-29)(KJV)

4 Therefore, when the Lord knew that the
Pharisees had heard that Jesus made and
baptized more disciples than John [2] (though
Jesus Himself did not baptize, His disciples),
[3] He left Judea and departed again to Galilee.
[4] But He needed to go through Samaria.
[5] So He came to a city of Samaria which is
called Sychar, near the plot of ground that
Jacob gave to his son Joseph. [6] Now Jacob's
well was there. Jesus therefore, being wearied
from *His* journey, sat thus by the well. It was

about the sixth hour.
7 A woman of Samaria came to draw water.
Jesus said to her, "Give Me a drink." 8 For His
disciples had gone away into the city to buy
food.
9 Then the woman of Samaria said to Him,
"How is it that You, being a Jew, ask a drink
from me, a Samaritan woman?" For Jews have
no dealings with Samaritans.
10 Jesus answered and said to her, "If you
knew the gift of God, and who it is who says to
you, 'Give Me a drink,' you would have asked
Him, and He would have given you living
water."
11 The woman said to Him, "Sir, You have
nothing to draw with, and the well is deep.
Where then do You get that living water?
12 Are You greater than our father Jacob, who
gave us the well, and drank from it himself, as
well as his sons and his livestock?"
13 Jesus answered and said to her, "Whoever
drinks of this water will thirst again, 14 but
whoever drinks of the water that I shall give
him will never thirst. But the water that I shall
give him will become in him a fountain of
water springing up into everlasting life."

15 The woman said to Him, "Sir, give me this
water, that I may not thirst, nor come here to
draw."
16 Jesus said to her, "Go, call your husband,
and come here."
17 The woman answered and said, "I have no
husband."
Jesus said to her, "You have well said, 'I
have no husband,' 18 for you have had five
husbands, and the one whom you now have is
not your husband; in that, you spoke truly."
19 The woman said to Him, "Sir, I perceive
that You are a prophet. 20 Our fathers
worshiped on this mountain, and you *Jews* say
that in Jerusalem is the place where one ought
to worship."
21 Jesus said to her, "Woman, believe Me, the
hour is coming when you will neither on this
mountain nor in Jerusalem, worship the Father.
22 You worship what you do not know; we
know what we worship, for salvation is of the
Jews. 23 But the hour is coming, and now is,
when the true worshipers will worship the
Father in spirit and truth; for the Father is
seeking such to worship Him. 24 God *is* Spirit,
and those who worship Him must worship in

spirit and truth."
25 The woman said to Him, "I know that
Messiah is coming" (who is called Christ).
"When He comes, He will tell us all things."
26 Jesus said to her, "I who speak to you am
He."

The Whitened Harvest

27 And at this *point* His disciples came, and
they marveled that He talked with a woman;
yet no one said, "What do You seek?" or,
"Why are You talking with her?"
28 The woman then left her waterpot, went
her way into the city, and said to the men,
29 "Come, see a Man who told me all things
that I ever did. Could this be the Christ?"
30 Then they went out of the city and came to
Him.

Be Proactive, be brave

(Luke 8:43-45)(NKJV)

43 Now a certain woman, had a flow of blood
for twelve years, who had spent all of her
livelihood on physicians and could not be
healed by any, 44 came from behind and
touched the border of his garment. And
immediately her flow of blood stopped.
45 And Jesus said, "Who touched Me?"
When all denied it, Peter and those with him
said, "Master, the multitudes throng and press
You, and You say, "Who touched Me?"
46 But Jesus said, "Somebody touched Me,
for I perceived power going out from Me." 47
Now when the woman saw that she was not
hidden, she came trembling; and falling down
before Him, she declared to Him in the
presence of all the people the reason she had
touched Him and how she was healed
immediately.
48 And he said to her, "Daughter, be of good
cheer; your faith has made you well. Go in
peace."

Only a woman could, and she did

(Mathew 9:20-22)

20 And suddenly, a woman who had a flow of
blood for twelve years came from behind and
touched the hem of his garment. 21 For she said
to herself, "If I may touch His garment,f I shall
be made well."
22 But Jesus turned around, and when He saw
her, He said, "Be of good cheer, daughter;
your faith has made you well." And the
woman was made well from that hour.

(Mark 5:25)

25 Now a certain woman had a flow of blood
for twelve years, 26and had suffered many
things from many physicians. She had spent all
that she had and was no better, but rather grew
worse. 27 When she heard about Jesus, she
came behind Him in the crowd and touched
His garment. 28 For she said, “If only I may
touch His clothes, I shall be made well.”

Make People Accountable

Now a certain *man* was sick, Lazarus of
Bethany, the town of Mary and her sister
Martha. [2] It was *that* Mary who anointed the
Lord with fragrant oil and wiped His feet with
her hair, whose brother Lazarus was sick.
[3] Therefore the sisters sent to Him, saying,
"Lord, behold, he whom You love is sick."
[4] When Jesus heard *that,* He said, "This
sickness is not unto death, but for the glory of
God, that the Son of God may be glorified
through it."
[5] Now Jesus loved Martha and her sister and
Lazarus. [6] So, when He heard that he was sick,
He stayed two more days in the place where
He was. [7] Then after this, He said to *the*
disciples, "Let us go to Judea again."
[8] *The* disciples said to Him, "Rabbi, lately the
Jews sought to stone You, and are You going
there again?"
[9] Jesus answered, "Are there not twelve hours
in the day? If anyone walks in the day, he does
not stumble, because he sees the light of this
world. [10] But if one walks in the night, he

stumbles, because the light is not in him."
11 These things He said, and after that, He said
to them, "Our friend Lazarus sleeps, but I go
that I may wake him up."
12 Then His disciples said, "Lord, if he sleeps
he will get well." 13 However, Jesus spoke of
his death, but they thought that He was
speaking about taking rest in sleep.
14 Then Jesus said to them plainly, "Lazarus
is dead. 15 And I am glad for your sakes that I
was not there, that you may believe.
Nevertheless, let us go to him."
16 Then Thomas, who is called the Twin, said
to his fellow disciples, "Let us also go, that we
may die with Him."

I Am the Resurrection and the Life

17 So when Jesus came, He found that he had
already been in the tomb four days. 18 Now
Bethany was near Jerusalem, about two
miles[a] away. 19 And many of the Jews had
joined the women around Martha and Mary, to
comfort them concerning their brother.
20 Now Martha, as soon as she heard that
Jesus was coming, went and met Him, but
Mary was sitting in the house. 21 Now Martha
said to Jesus, "Lord, if You had been here, my

brother would not have died. 22 But even now I
know that whatever You ask of God, God will
give You."
23 Jesus said to her, "Your brother will rise
again."

www.ingramcontent.com/pod-product-compliance
Lightning Source LLC
LaVergne TN
LVHW050950080826
845145LV00004B/1455

* 9 7 8 0 9 9 1 2 2 1 8 7 5 *